HOW TO PREPARE FOR, HIRE, AND MANAGE A KICK ASS VIRTUAL ASSISTANT

Charlene L. Ruell

© 2020 Charlene L. Ruell

Charlene L Ruell
How to Prepare for, Hire, and Manage a Kick Ass Virtual Assistant

Self-Published
Cover and Text Design by Charlene L. Ruell

ISBN 9798587376267

This book would not have been possible without the most amazing clients I could ask for!

You each inspire me everyday and I am eternally thankful to have you in my life: Veronica, Zohe, Kala, Mary, Shelly, Sue, and Marianne.

A GUIDE TO THE GUIDE

Introduction ... 9

Believing You Can Hire Someone ... 13

Tasks ... 17

Creating a Kick Ass Ad ... 23

Where to Find Someone ... 27

How to Properly Vet Applications ... 29

Pre-interview Contact ... 35

Interview Questions ... 39

Conducting an Interview ... 43

Testing Your Applicants ... 47

Making a Final Decision ... 49

Post-interview Contact ... 51

Contracts and Agreements (including payment and terms) ... 53

Business Manual ... 57

Orientation ... 61

Communication ... 63

How to Effectively Manage Someone Virtually ... 67

INTRODUCTION

Before we dive into the exciting world of virtual assistants and most importantly, finding you one, a short introduction.

As someone who has been working in administration for what amounts to a very long time (this is the equivalent to a long time ago in a galaxy far far away), I've been both the manager and the assistant – with varying degrees of success. From being told on more than one occasion, that I was the best manager that person had ever had, to being the one with the slightly fractured boss who was put in awkward situations. I know the good, the bad, and the ugly.

There did come a time when I decided to move on from that life and start something new. I needed this to be both different and better. I would choose who I worked with, helping those that needed it most and thus, I opened my own creative agency specifically for small businesses. Now, I cater to small businesses – most are single person operations – that need a leg up. In most cases I work from 1-5 hours a week, per client, doing anything from Social Media Management to Website Design.

I love my new life and my amazing clients. Then I decided to go a step further and tell others about this and here we are.

This guide is meant to help anyone who is pulling their hair out, overwhelmed, or who just needs that one thing taken off their plate. You know that thing that is always there and never gets done because you never have the time? Yeah, that one. We're going to find someone to help you with that. It's going to be life changing.

I call this a guide because that is what it is. It is a tool to lead you in the right direction, tell you the left and right turns to make, but it is not a self-driving car. You still need to provide the power, step on that accelerator, and complete the steps necessary to meet your goal.

In these pages you will find guidance and activities to help you on your way. Each activity has a workbook page at the back of this book (you can download the pdf version too, if you wish) and there are also accompanying video lessons available to you for free. Perhaps you learn better when listening – not a problem!

You also have access to me. Afterall, in putting this guide out in the world, I want you to be successful. Stuck on a certain step? Have a question about something that isn't covered? Please reach out!

I'm not going to lie; this will be quite a bit of work. It will also be hugely satisfying and in the end, will only help to improve the well-being of both yourself and your business.

Let's get started!

SECTION I
PREPARATION

BELIEVING YOU CAN HIRE SOMEONE

As a business owner you put an immense amount of energy into maintaining the everyday. There is no doubt that you have entertained the thought of cloning yourself — if there were only two of you, things would be so much easier! The benefit of the clone? It knows what you know, there isn't any training and there is no pesky process of hiring someone.

Unfortunately, this isn't a realistic option and, let's be honest, if it was, it wouldn't be affordable for most businesses.

Your next best option? Hiring someone.

Given that you have this book and are reading it, I'm guessing you aren't audibly groaning right now, as I would expect most people would when given this suggestion. The mere thought of what it takes to hire someone leads many entrepreneurs into the 'I can do it all' trap. Inevitably, they come out the other side overworked, stressed to the breaking point, and in need of a good year or two off. "If I only had help," they think, and the cycle begins again.

We are here to break that cycle my friends!

Now, more than ever, there are thousands, if not millions of freelancers who can help you do anything from data entry to finance. The ability to remote work has also made this option more viable for providers and more affordable for clients. Hiring someone is no longer a costly and time sucking activity— it can be quite fun!

First and foremost, put away your pre-conceived notion of what an assistant can do for you. Don't think of this as a full-time position or regular type of working relationship. You want to find someone and give them tasks that CREATE time for you. That's what this process is all about, ensuring you have more time — time to concentrate on the things that matter to you, time to invest in yourself, and time to breathe.

Perhaps you have been down this road before, and trust me, it happens all too often that you hire someone, thinking that you will finally have time to get to that list you've had for ages, but, managing them takes even more time away from you.

The secret? Hiring someone you trust and ensuring you give them tasks that are small, manageable, and that don't require loads of supervision. For instance, in a mere two hours per week, you could have someone send out a newsletter for you and schedule 5-7 days' worth of social media. In just two hours.

If you are thinking this isn't plausible and you won't possibly find anyone to work for you for only two hours, you are incorrect. My own clients vary in hours per week from 2 – 10 and there are many more freelancers like myself throughout the world. The key to this process and to finding someone to fit your needs is being open, honest, and upfront.

You can't do it all, you do need help, and yes, you can find someone amazing!

TASKS

The biggest part of hiring someone is getting organized — figuring out exactly what they can do for you is one of the biggest steps you will take. Not only are you organizing what needs to be done within your business (a frightening task to be sure), you are also preparing to hand over control to someone else. For those of you in the I can do it all zone, just a warning that you may have a little trouble letting go. I promise, it will be worth it!

Ready to begin your journey? Let's get to it!

Creating your task list doesn't have to be a super intensive project. Think about the everyday running of your business and start there. It may be helpful to make an overall list of recurring tasks and then discern those items that you might like to shift to someone else. Typically, recurring tasks are the easiest to shift to an assistant, as your new hire will only become more proficient over time. Remember, you want to choose tasks that are small, manageable, and don't require a lot of supervision.

Alternatively, you may find it easier to make a list of things you don't like to do, as a jumping off point — the brain tends to retain negative thought more often, especially if you do something on a regular basis. However, it is important that you not fall into the 'grunt work' mentality. It is vital that you treat your assistant, even when you haven't hired them, with respect. They will need to see the value in their work and feel that they are contributing to your business. They are, essentially, a partner.

It is also helpful to think about the future. You aren't hiring someone for a one-off project; this is a relationship you hope to maintain over time — plan for it. Though you can't predict the future, make a wish list of things that you would like to accomplish in the next few years. From my perspective as a provider, I always ask potential clients what their business plans are for the future. It is important for me to know that they are looking ahead and that those plans include me. If all else fails, you can turn your wish list into tasks that you and your new assistant take on as you have time and budget.

Most importantly, when making your list, remember that the purpose in hiring your assistant is to CREATE time for you. These tasks are serving an overall purpose — ensure that the items you are selecting, help you in achieving your goal.

HOURS

With your task list underway, you next need to determine how many hours you might be able to commit to someone each week. The number of hours doesn't need to be consistent with the items on your list, but it should have some overlap. For instance, you don't want to give someone a task that is bigger than the number of hours you can provide, but you could allow time for tasks to be broken into stages or done over time. Tasks may also fluctuate and keep in mind that most likely not every task will need to be completed each week.

It is important at this stage to remember that you are hiring an expert to do this, this isn't how much time this task normally takes YOU. You want to estimate the number of hours that someone who is proficient, would ultimately spend completing an item. Be realistic and manage expectations — you want to allow enough time for your hire to do the task and do it well.

Another thing to keep in mind, is that your overall hours don't need to be a single figure — feel free to give yourself a range. Begin with an absolute minimum and then think about a maximum that fits in with your budget.

When estimating your billable hours, also ensure you add in time for maintenance — things like calls, research, and items that will help you and your assistant manage your time together. For instance, if you are someone who needs to talk it out or check in often, build in at least a half an hour for a weekly call.

Ensuring you have an accurate picture of your overall need, will help you to be open and honest about the work that will be taking place. Plan now, to ensure things go smoothly down the road.

BUDGET

The last step of the preparation section, is, you guessed it, budget.

This part is tricky, as rates may vary depending on your tasks and who you hire. However, don't be afraid to be flexible with your figures. If someone has a higher rate, but has more skills and is more efficient, then you may only need to commit your minimum hours.

Consider what your business budget might allow — first in a whole number and then hourly. For instance, you have $200 in your budget per month. If someone is asking $25/hour, then you can afford 8 hours of time a month or roughly 2 hours per week.

At this point, you may be asking why the budget wasn't considered before the hours. After all, it is hard to commit time to someone if you can't pay them for it. However, it is important that you figure out your hourly need first, even though your budget may say otherwise, as this is a good way to gauge how much work you have overall.

You may find that you need to start out slow at first and as your business income increases, so will your budget and ability to give your hire more hours and tasks.

ACTIVITY

As a reminder, in the back of this book you will find the workbook for all of the activities. As a book lover, I get that not everyone wants to permanently scribble on a page you have only one copy of. For this reason, you will find links that lead to both printable and fillable PDF pages for each activity.

There are three tasks for this activity.

1. Make a list of tasks that you currently don't have time for or those that you are thinking of implementing in the future. These can be as specific (creating graphics for social media) or as vague (data entry) as you want. Try to come up with at least 5.

2. Assign your tasks an estimated time for completion — remember this can be a range. Figure out your overall weekly need.

3. Estimate your overall budget and the number of hours that you might be able to fund. This can also be a range, as you will find varying pay rates and skill level in your search.

SECTION II
HIRING

CREATING A KICK ASS AD

Congratulations, you made it to section two — give yourself some applause (also known as an introvert high-five)!

We've come a long way in a short time! You have created a task list, estimated your need, and settled on a budget — now let's hire you a kick ass assistant!

The first and, I'm sure, most obvious step, is to create an advertisement. However, instead of writing it for YOU, you are going to write it for your potential hire. You want a kick ass assistant? You need to have the right kind of ad to attract them.

As we walk through these steps, we'll build a fictional ad for Deanne the Magician. Deanne is dynamic, fun, loves sequins, and takes her profession seriously— the magician's code is everything!

Let's start at the beginning. You want to hook your applicants with a catchy headline that embodies not only the work, but who you want to do it. Utilize keywords associated with your brand and give them a fun twist. You aren't a corporate entity offering some stuffy job, you are looking for a dynamic individual to work with you and your business.

For Deanne, who has a bit of trouble staying organized, we might use a headline that reads: Organizationally Challenged Magician Seeks Wizard Virtual Assistant.

This headline tells perspective applicants that most likely, they will be helping Deanne organize and that she is looking for a person who is efficient, quick, and knows their tasks so well, it's almost like magic.

After the headline, you want to include a short summary of your ad. Take the lead from your headline, give a few more details, and dive a bit more into who you are and what your business is. For those applicants that may simply be skimming, this is your second chance to make an impression (or to weed out this who aren't interested).

Make your ad dynamic and fun. Use your mission, values, and ensure that you represent your brand.

> Do you consider yourself a wizard? Can you organize the seemingly unorganizable? Deanne the magician is looking for a fun, dynamic, and truly magical individual to join her team! Help keep this sparkling entertainer's lifestyle on track by tracking her bookings, potential leads, and rehearsal schedule.

Follow up your summary with an about me blurb, before diving into the list of potential tasks and requirements.

> Deanne is a seasoned magician that uses her signature vintage style to dazzle audiences around the world! She loves bringing joy to the faces of those most skeptical and wowing children of all ages.

When listing potential tasks be honest, upfront, and transparent.

As an experienced Wizard, you would be assisting Deanne with:

- Maintaining her performance schedule;
- Fielding potential leads;
- Tracking her rehearsal schedule and potential conflicts;
- Future projects as needed.

Preferably you are:

- A pro at organization;
- Someone with an excellent phone and email demeanor;
- Familiar with the Honeybook CRM;
- In the Central or Pacific Time Zones;
- Respectful of the magician's code.

Depending on where you are posting the ad (that's next up ya'll!), you may also include contact information and/or other requirements as needed.

I'm sure some of you are thinking — hey, wait a minute, didn't we leave a few things out? Gold star for you, my friend! Two things we didn't add in, our hours and our budget. Why?

The hours and your budget may fluctuate depending on who you are hiring. Remember, this isn't a traditional job posting. Some sites will allow you to categorize your listing under a range, such as 1-10, 10-15, or 20+; however, this is typically not required. You can include your minimum hours, but always be careful to manage expectations — be clear about the frequency (weekly/monthly) and that this number is subject to change based on budget and skill.

Creating a dynamic ad and being clear about your needs and expectations will ensure you attract the right potential hires. You will increase your chances of finding an amazing individual who will continue to stay with your business for as long as you need them.

ACTIVITY

As a reminder, in the back of this book you will find the workbook for all of the activities. As a book lover, I get that not everyone wants to permanently scribble on a page you have only one copy of. For this reason, you will find links that lead to both printable and fillable PDF pages for each activity.

Creating a fun and dynamic ad that is geared toward who you want to hire is key. Use the example and the tools in the workbook to create your own ad.

WHERE TO FIND SOMEONE

With your ad in hand, you now need it in front of your potential hires. Finding out where these fine folk are, is the next step in your journey.

Let's start off with the easiest option — ask those you know. This can be a friend, colleague, or someone in the same social media group as you. There are several benefits to exploring this avenue first. You get a recommendation right away from someone you trust, the recommender will most likely know that person's strengths, and they will likely be able to give an indication of whether you would click.

There are two important tips related to the clicking concept — 1. If you don't click with someone or feel that they aren't right for you, don't push it. It's very much a round peg, square hole scenario, which leads me to two. 2. Invest the time now, to ensure things go smoothly down the road. I have been in too many hiring scenarios where someone is put in place quickly, just to fill a need. They rarely last and will cause you to lose even more time starting a new search.

What if you don't have any recommendations or you don't feel the ones that you have been given are right for you?

There are a few options for resources; however, I would highly recommend staying away from sites that cater to anyone looking for regular employment or work — sites like indeed and craigslist. You are looking for someone for a very specific purpose, thus I highly recommend a specific site. My top pick for hiring a freelancer is Upwork.

Upwork has been around for a while and is continuing to evolve as the freelance industry does. You can search here by task, region, specialty, etc. This kind of resource will also give you built in tools for paying your hire, rating them, and contracts —something a basic employment site will not. Upwork in particular, also requires freelancers to bid on jobs with purchased credits, which ensures you are only getting those people that are interested in your position.

There are additional sites — freelancer.com and fiver.com — though I cannot vouch for them or the quality of applicant they can provide. Be cautious about where you post and do a little research about the company and the talent they attract before doing so.

Knowing where and where not to look for a potential assistant can help you avoid uninterested applicants, insincere inquiries, and funds spent on unfruitful resources.

HOW TO PROPERLY VET APPLICATIONS

Your ad is posted, applicants are interested, but how do you choose who is right for you? How do you guarantee that you are hiring someone that will stick with you?

When vetting applications, there are quite a few things to look out for that will help you as you start to look through applications — even before you get to the applicant's qualifications.

The number one complaint I hear when interviewing potential clients, is that during a previous experience, they thought they were hiring an individual, but got stuck working with multiple assistants an agency. This is very common in the freelance world — to have a network of virtual assistants under one banner. If you think about it from the agency perspective, it's very smart. With multiple people and specialties, you become a one stop shop for anything a client might need. From the client's perspective, agencies can be frustrating. You are often shuffled from person to person and never given much of a chance to build a working relationship or the all-important flow that eventually develops between a client and assistant. It may be that you don't mind this working style; however more often than not, a solo-peneur will choose to look elsewhere. If you think this is something you would like to avoid, pay close attention to wording such as we/us instead of I/me. Also, examine the business name and ratings. If the ratings refer to multiple people within the feedback, then you are most likely dealing with an agency. Don't hesitate to double check when contacting your potential Virtual Assistant. If they do work for an agency, verify that they will be the sole person handling your work and that they have a viable plan in place for a handover, should circumstances change.

The next big hurdle is time zones. At another point in my life, I worked internationally and learned to work around even the most challenging of time differences — I am on the west coast, our department assistant was in Australia. When I opened my business, I promised myself that I would only take on clients on the west coast — juggling meetings at odd hours and having less control over direct communication can be exhausting. Like the agency issue, I've heard a lot of feedback from potential clients regarding time zones as well. It can work, but this is something you absolutely must keep in mind. Perhaps you live on the east coast but do most of your work during the evening — this would be compatible with hiring someone in the central, mountain, or pacific time zones, as well as eastern. Think about when you do your work and how much contact you need to have during the working day with your hire.

The last item to look at before diving into the application itself, is bidding. As I mentioned before, the system at UpWork and most other freelance sites, works on a bidding system — just like you would have a contractor bid to work on your house. Freelancers submit a response to your ad, their bid — a potential hourly or project rate — and answer any questions you might have posed.

Looking at things from the provider side, at Upwork in particular, potential applicants can see what the client's previous pay rates were and the system suggests a bid rate based on this. It will also show an applicant the current range of bids. When viewing these numbers, I was consistently taken aback by the number of clients who hired only at the lowest rate. To make the relationship work and to ensure it is a lasting one, it is essential that you respect your potential hire. Don't go for the lowest bid, because it's the lowest, go for the person you feel is the most qualified and is the best fit — rates are often negotiable.

Alternatively, pay attention to high bidders as well. If someone is telling you that it will cost $100 an hour to manage your social media, they should be amazing at what they do. More times than not, these freelancers are inflating their bid to make themselves seem more qualified — don't trust this. Vet your applicants and find out who is truly qualified.

While there is no perfect formula for vetting qualifications, as each applicant and position requirements will vary, there are some best practices to help you and red flags to avoid. After all, finding someone who can do the work and do it well, is an essential part to making sure your hire will be long-term.

There are many ways to evaluate and rate your potential applicant's qualifications. Regardless of the way it is done, it is essential that you keep your system consistent, organized, and fair. You will need to refer to each application several times and need to be confident about your ultimate decision.

Your potential hires will most likely come to you via email and it can be hard to organize enquiries into a digestible format. Start by separating your applicants from the rest of your email — either sorting them into a folder, saving them to an external source (such as Dropbox or Google Drive), or if you are a tactile person, printing them out.

From there, you can begin to evaluate skill and fit and narrow down the field.

Starting with skill, look at each application and ask:

- Does this applicant meet the minimum requirements?
- How much experience do they have (in years or months) with the specific tasks you need assistance with?
- How much experience do they have (in years or months) being a Virtual Assistant or working remotely?
- Do they have other skills or experience that might be beneficial to your business in the future?

A good practice is to record responses to these questions in some manner. Relying on your memory can often be unreliable and lead to confusing various applicants. One of the best ways to keep track of qualifications is through creating a spreadsheet or ratings document. For instance, creating a column for each category and assigning a score based upon your impression.

Name	Minimum Requirements	Task Experience	VA Experience	Other Experience	Notes
Sally	4	3	4	2	Pacific Time Zone

You can then easily total your scores and have an accurate picture of your top applicants and who you would like to move to the next round. Just remember to be consistent about your scoring and what your various values mean.

Alternatively, forgoing a number system and recording notes about each applicant would also be equally effective (especially for those of us not great with numbers or spreadsheets). You can quickly review each person without having to dive back into each application.

Aside from the main qualification questions, what else do you need to be cognizant of during application evaluation?

Inevitably, there will be those who are doing this as a temporary pit stop on the way to another full-time gig elsewhere. Starting to work with someone and leaving a few weeks later is not cool, but a lot of people still do it. Be sure to pay close attention to the work history, especially if they've made a sudden recent jump into freelancing or have no experience at all. Make a note of it and ensure to ask about it if the applicant makes it to the interview phase. Also, don't be afraid to be forward about wanting someone for the long term. If you continue to have doubts, even after speaking with them, add a term clause into the contract and be sure they are willing to make a commitment in writing.

Evaluating the work experience in general, is also a good idea to assess if your new hire is a flight risk. How long have they spent at each position? Do they job jump or are there long periods of unemployment they haven't explained?

Looking at the educational accomplishments of each applicant can also be helpful, but unless you included a requirement in your ad, this should not be a deciding factor in your decision. In particular, assess if they have a degree or certificate that specializes in the type of work you need. Perhaps their degree doesn't relate to the tasks but does relate to your field of business. Having a larger scope of knowledge about a field can be particularly beneficial and help to get more pointed work off the ground quicker.

Similarly, try to make an initial fit assessment. Are there items present in the application that signal the applicant might be a good fit? If you need someone detail oriented, are the application materials well written and thorough? Looking for someone with a good sense of humor? Examine their stylistic and language choices. You can also use practices like these to weed out those who are not a good fit. Anyone that you aren't sure of, but who does pass your initial skill evaluation, you can either interview or to save time and energy, send them a secondary questionnaire that addresses your concerns.

Once you have done your assessments and narrowed down the field, you may find that there are promising applicants that meet some of your needs, but not all. If this is the case, it is always good to remain open to hiring multiple people. There are unicorns out there who are multi-talented, but they are rare. Breaking up the work can be a great way to retain those who are experts in a particular specialty and ensure you are getting the best people for the job.

Thoroughly vetting your potential hires is key to ensuring that you are partnering with the right Virtual Assistant and that the relationship will last.

ACTIVITY

As a reminder, in the back of this book you will find the workbook for all of the activities. As a book lover, I get that not everyone wants to permanently scribble on a page you have only one copy of. For this reason, you will find links that lead to both printable and fillable PDF pages for each activity.

Devise an evaluation matrix and system that allows you record, track, and evaluate your applicants. Ensure it allows you refer to it quickly and easily and above all else, that it makes your job easier, not more difficult.

PRE-INTERVIEW CONTACT

You have now vetted your applicants and narrowed down the field — congratulations, you are ready to interview!

As a rule of thumb, always interview, even if someone is recommended to you. I would also encourage you to hold a video interview — there's nothing quite like measuring a face to face reaction.

But before you jump into chatting with potential hires, there are a few things that need to be prepared.

First and foremost, you will need a way — that is beneficial for both you and the interviewee — to schedule a time to speak. Depending on the number of interviews you are holding, there are a few methods you can employ. My preferred method for scheduling interviews is with Calendly (calendly.com), an application that checks against your existing calendars for availability. You can input a schedule, add your preferences for lead time, number of days in advance an appointment can be made, and other details.

The system then creates time slots that your interviewees can self schedule — all you need to do is send them a link.

If the thought of setting up a whole new system sounds exhausting (trust me, I get it), then you can always just email your availability out and schedule on a first come, first served, basis.

Either way, after you decide how you want to handle scheduling, you will need to communicate with your interviewees. Your message should be informative, thorough, and give the recipient all the details they need to know about the process moving forward. At minimum, you should include:

- An obvious subject line to ensure it catches the applicant's attention
- A greeting thanking the applicant for their application
- Details about the interview, how to schedule it, where and how it will take place, and how long it is expected to last
- Items that need to be provided in the meantime (if you are asking for a resume or CV, additional questionnaire, etc)
- Additional details about the overall hiring process, to set expectations moving forward

You can expect there to be some drop off during this stage of the process. Inevitably, an email address won't work, an applicant won't respond, or they will have already found work with another client. Please don't feel that this is a reflection upon you or your business.

The communication may also provide you with further insights into your applicants. The behaviors they exhibit are an indicator of how they will function when you are working together. How quickly do they respond to messages? Is the communication thorough or do they need to be prodded for additional information? Make notes as necessary and use these indicators as part of your overall decision process.

Though it may not seem important, ensuring proper

communication throughout the pre-interview process is essential to getting the working relationship started on the right foot.

ACTIVITY

As a reminder, in the back of this book you will find the workbook for all of the activities. As a book lover, I get that not everyone wants to permanently scribble on a page you have only one copy of. For this reason, you will find links that lead to both printable and fillable PDF pages for each activity.

Create a template message that you will use during your interview communications. Ensure you have the minimum components included and try to make the content as dynamic and engaging as you can.

INTERVIEW QUESTIONS

While you are reaching out to your applicants for an interview, you should also be preparing your interview questions. Though you can ask some spontaneous questions or follow-ups, you should have a list of overall guiding questions prepared — 10 is typically a great number to shoot for.

Questions should be geared toward vetting skills and making an assessment for overall fit. This is your chance to get any questions answered or concerns addressed from the application phase.

At least three of your questions should explore the applicant's background, including and beyond what was included within the materials they submitted. These questions should seek to fill in any blanks, provide you with a clear idea of previous experiences, and give the applicant a chance to introduce themselves (and their personality) to you.

An additional three questions should focus on skill. What are the tasks you want your Virtual Assistant help with? What is their experience in these areas? Don't be afraid to present a scenario and ask what process they would use, how long it would take, and what they think the overall impact to your business would be.

The final set of three questions should guide you in finding out if the applicant is the right fit for you. Utilize these as an opportunity to explore how the applicant works, what their expectations are, and how the two of you might communicate over particular issues. Proposing "what would you do" questions can be effective — such as "What would you do … if someone asked you to do something you felt was wrong"?

The final question can be reserved for the applicant to ask you questions. There are differing schools of thought on whether this is an effective use of time; however, from my perspective, if the applicant has thoroughly prepared, they should have at minimum some basic questions about your business. If they don't it can be a good indicator of overall disinterest and that perhaps, the applicant is not in it for the long haul.

Overall, be bold in your questions and don't be shy about asking about what you need to know. Avoid fluff questions that don't give you valuable information (If you were a flavor of ice cream, what would you be?). My all-time favorite question to ask is "What's the biggest misconception people have about you?" I think you'll find it typically yields some honest and surprising results.

Ensuring you ask the right questions during the interview stage will give you a plethora of valuable information needed to make a final decision. You will ultimately have a more in-depth picture of your applicant, their skills, and if they are the right fit for you and your business.

ACTIVITY

As a reminder, in the back of this book you will find the workbook for all of the activities. As a book lover, I get that not everyone wants to permanently scribble on a page you have only one copy of. For this reason, you will find links that lead to both printable and fillable PDF pages for each activity.

Create a set of 10 guiding questions for your interview, including 3 focusing on background, 3 on skill, 3 on fit, and the final one for the applicant to pose questions.

CONDUCTING AN INTERVIEW

With your interview questions in hand and your applicants scheduled in, you are ready to conduct your interviews!

Interviewing can be absolutely nerve wrecking for both the interviewer and interviewee. Many interviewers utilize specific tactics, most with the intention of asserting dominance or power over the person they are speaking with. For instance, a former boss always lowered the lights in his office and kept a very solemn expression. Even though he was the least threatening person, those he interviewed noted that he was very intimidating. While I wouldn't recommend doing this for the type of role you are interviewing for, it was very effective for his situation and made his applicants realize the gravity of their situation.

Taking an interview tactic like this into consideration, think about how you want your relationship with your assistant to begin. Ensure you maintain an approachable demeanor, be open to the conversation, and situate yourself as more of a guide than someone with absolute control.

The biggest way that you can ensure your applicant feels welcome and heard, is to practice active listening. Active listening is a technique you can employ in any situation but is incredibly effective in work environments. How do you do it?

Active listening relies on the observation of your interviewee's behavior and body language, and your ability to interpret and adjust. Use these prompts to help you during your interview to get the best results:

1. Keep your goals in mind
2. Focus on the interviewee when you aren't speaking and keep your portion of the conversation limited
3. Be open and guide the conversation – don't project yourself as the overlord interviewer
4. After the applicant is finished speaking, summarize what you hear before you head to a follow-up or the next question
5. Don't be afraid to ask additional questions if you need more detail; however, be sure you encourage information, don't force it
6. Stay positive, encourage, and show your interest

Now that you have a mindset for the interview itself, let's discuss how you will conduct it.

First, the technology piece. As you will be interacting with your new assistant virtually and they may be some distance from you, I would recommend conducting the interview this way as well. There are a few options available to aid you in connecting for the interview. I would highly recommend that you utilize the same option that you will use to communicate on an ongoing basis. Doing this will clue you in to any difficulties that your potential assistant might have with the technology.

There are three video conferencing options that I would

recommend – all of them free. If you are utilizing Upwork for your search, they offer resources such as a chat and video calls. While it is a convenient option for both parties involved, this option doesn't allow you a real-world environment outside of the Upwork space. I would compare it to a flight simulator vs actually flying. I have also experienced technical difficulties with the interface and consider myself extremely well versed in technology – utilize at your own risk.

Next up on the list is Zoom. Before everyone on the planet (literally) came to know Zoom as the definitive video calling software, it was used mostly by non-profits due to its low price point and plethora of call-in numbers. You can get an account for free and there is no cost for one-on-one calls; if you have two or more participants, free accounts are limited to a 45-minute call. As a bonus, Zoom integrates with various schedulers, such as Calendly, which we mentioned in the pre-interview contact section.

Another wonderful solution is Google Hangouts, also known as Google Meet for those with a GSuite account. The wonderful thing about Hangouts is that it integrates directly with your Google Calendar and Gmail natively – no setup required. Calendly also integrates with Google nicely, so you can have a seamless process.

Now that you have the tools to connect you, let's move on to the actual interview.

To start off on the right foot, send the applicant a short message before you begin, if you can. This serves as both a reminder of the appointment and reassures them that you are invested in the conversation.

When things begin, don't be afraid to have some light-hearted conversation first. I find that a simple ice breaker, such as asking about the weather or how their day was, is a great way to make them feel at ease. Then, gradually guide the conversation back to its intended purpose and give a short outline about how the interview will be structured – letting them know what they can expect, when. Providing an introduction of yourself, your company, and a brief summary of the job as well.

Armed with a proper mindset, a video conferencing tool, and ways to get started, you are now ready to tackle the first meeting with your applicants!

TESTING YOUR APPLICANTS

The interviews are over, you have met a lot of amazing people, and have a good idea of who you want to hire – the process is done, right? Not quite.

While you have read resumes, made evaluation matrixes, and asked questions in an interview, you still need to be 100% sure that you have the right fit. Someone can say they are an expert, but can they prove it? Can they do the work that you require?

The solution? Give them a test drive. Devise a short task to test their skills (and speed), ensuring the test is relevant to the skills you require. For instance, if you are looking for a Social Media person, given them 5 images and ask that they write sample posts for you with your brand in mind. This may be simple, but it will help to weed out those who aren't all they claim to be.

Providing a test for your applicants will not only help you in making your final decision but will also provide them with a glimpse into what the job will entail.

ACTIVITY

As a reminder, in the back of this book you will find the workbook for all of the activities. As a book lover, I get that not everyone wants to permanently scribble on a page you have only one copy of. For this reason, you will find links that lead to both printable and fillable PDF pages for each activity.

Devise a test for your applicants that evaluates the relevant skills you need. Ensure the test measures the aspects that are important to you, such as speed, creativity, and presentation.

MAKING A FINAL DECISION

It's nearly that time! You've done a lot of work to get to this point and you will soon be on your way to a great relationship with an amazing Virtual Assistant!

With the results of your test in, you should add the information about both the interview and the test to your overall notes or spreadsheet. By now, you inevitably have a good idea of who you want to hire. They have solid qualifications, interviewed well, and did a great job on the test – you've clicked!

If you haven't, don't be afraid to hold a second round of interviews or even to open the application process again. As I mentioned before, putting the time in now to ensure you have the right person, will save you time, money, and headache down the line.

If you have found your new Virtual Assistant, congrats! Let's take one final step to solidify this great match – asking for a professional reference. This may seem like something that is more traditionally job focused, but like the test drive, it will give you one last chance to discover elements that the applicant won't talk about.

Generally, most people know that asking for a reference is the last step before hiring and will have that expectation when you take this step. Though the assumption exists, it is best to manage expectations and not divulge if they are the top candidate – simply saying that this is a part of the process is enough.

There are many various ways that an applicant will provide a reference; however, even if it is on the application already, always ask for the information and contact the reference yourself — never accept a reference letter from the applicant directly.

When contacting the reference, be aware that legally, there may be specific questions that you cannot ask or information that cannot be given. This will often vary by state, country, or previous employer. Ensure you check what is applicable both in your locality and that of your potential hire.

The results of your reference check will, hopefully, reveal that you were correct in your evaluation. If, perchance, the check reveals something that you find questionable, be open with your applicant about it. Don't be afraid to have a call with them to discuss your concerns and how you might overcome any issues. This is, after all, the beginning of a working relationship. You need to be able to work through potential problems together.

Completing the reference check, you are now ready to let your potential hire know the great news – you are ready to work together! We will cover what you need to tell them in the next section.

POST-INTERVIEW CONTACT

Yes! This is the moment you have been waiting for and all your hard work has paid off! You have found your person and it is time to let them know!

It is best to contact your new hire first, in the case that they do not accept the offer, you can move to your next choice. However, before we get to those details, remember that you had many other applicants and they deserve to hear from you as well. Honestly, one of my biggest pet peeves when interviewing potential clients is never hearing from them. Ensure you remember that you aren't the only one who put time and energy into this process – always let everyone know the outcome. Creating a simple template will save loads of time and help you get through the list quickly. Be kind, courteous, and ensure you thank them for their time.

When delivering the good news to your new Virtual Assistant, there are a few ways you can go about it. By email, by phone, or by video call or any combination that might work best. Often, a video or phone call might take time to setup and schedule, therefore, sending them an email of congratulations and scheduling a time to talk about next steps is often best. This will also give them time to process the news and ask you more thoughtful and relevant questions.

Remember that the post-interview contact is the first impression of your new working relationship with someone and for those that didn't make it, their last impression of you. Ensuring that your messages are thoughtful and contain the correct information will get you started on the right foot.

ACTIVITY

As a reminder, in the back of this book you will find the workbook for all of the activities. As a book lover, I get that not everyone wants to permanently scribble on a page you have only one copy of. For this reason, you will find links that lead to both printable and fillable PDF pages for each activity.

Create two templates for your post-interview follow-up – one for your new hire and one for those that didn't make the cut. Make the letters 2-3 paragraphs and be kind, courteous, and always thank them for their time (yes, even your new hire). For your new hire, carefully outline the next steps you want to take – scheduling a follow-up call, settling on a start date, and of course verifying a pay rate and contract.

CONTRACTS AND AGREEMENTS (INCLUDING PAYMENT AND TERMS)

Congrats on your new hire! There is just one more step to complete before you lock them in and you being your new journey together.

Ensuring there is a contract between you and your Virtual Assistant is a vital step in the process. Working without a contract or written agreement, can open you and your business to liability and does not provide you with leverage if you are subject to legal action. Always be prepared, you never know what may happen.

In some cases, hires may have their own contracts and systems that they prefer use. Be sure to ask as part of your follow-up call or conversation. In my case, I use a tool that combines invoicing and contracts, so I prefer to utilize my own contracts.

Regardless of who manages the contract, it should always be presented to both parties for review and revision before signing.

At minimum, the contract or agreement should mention both parties' legal names (for you this means the name or DBA you operate under), legal addresses, and job description or a short list of expected duties (you can take this from your job description). These details provide the basis of your working relationship and demonstrate basic expectations.

Additionally, the more information you add, the more your working relationship is defined and laid out for both parties. A clause on payment terms can spell out when you are billed (bi-weekly, monthly, etc.), what forms of payment are accepted, and the pay rate. Term expectations can be added to define if this is this a limited contract with an end date, if there will be a probationary period, or at the least, the start date of your hire. Similarly, a termination clause provides both parties with the requirements for severing the relationship, such as a notice period and how any pending payments or expenses will be handled. Last, an Intellectual Property clause will define who owns the work that is produced and what is to be done with it at the end of the working relationship.

Though this is quite a bit of detail to go into, the more information provided at the outset, the clearer your relationship will be.

In the same vein as the contract, you can opt to have your Virtual Assistant sign a Non-Disclosure Agreement (NDA), especially if you work in an industry that is prone to intense competition or trade secrets. An NDA is in no way required but can serve to provide you with an extra layer of protection if you deem it necessary.

Taking the time to build a contract with your new hire will ensure each of you has agreed to the details of your working relationship in writing. Think of it as the first project you take on together!

ACTIVITY

As a reminder, in the back of this book you will find the workbook for all of the activities. As a book lover, I get that not everyone wants to permanently scribble on a page you have only one copy of. For this reason, you will find links that lead to both printable and fillable PDF pages for each activity.

Create a template for a contract and an NDA (if you deem that one is necessary), using the information above. You can also find examples of complete contracts easily with an internet search and may get more ideas for additional elements to add. Second, create a list of preferences for yourself (such as paying bi-weekly) that you can use as the basis for your conversation with your new hire.

SECTION III

MANAGING

BUSINESS MANUAL

Whew – it's been quite the journey to get here! Welcome to Section Three! Take a moment to catch your breath and revel in the success you have had on hiring the best Virtual Assistant EVER!

In this section we will chat about all the things you can do to be the best manager and foster an amazing relationship with the newest member of your team.

In general, it takes a full year for most new hires to fully adjust their positions. This is the point when tasks and ways of working together become the most productive. In some cases, you may not have a year, if you are taking on someone for a specific term or project. Most likely, regardless of time, you also want to bring your new hire up to speed as quickly as possible. What then, is the best way to ensure that this happens? Hands down, the most essential tool in your management arsenal, is to create a Business Manual.

A Business Manual is pretty much what it sounds like – a

manual for your business. This master document contains all the information that anyone working with you might need to know. The content is solely reliant upon your business needs and operation – there are no requirements for what you need to add. Take some time to think about what you do in your day-to-day, what is most essential to your business, and what are the things that will be most helpful to a Virtual Assistant.

The manual should be well organized and easy to navigate. If someone is looking for information, you don't want them spending ages to find it. Dividing it into sections or tabs is helpful, as is a clickable Table of Contents for any electronic versions.

While there are no hard and fast rules for what you should include, you might consider adding sections related to the following:

- Basic information such as your business address, hours, preferred contact information for various aspects, and information on how you like to work.
- Your Mission & Values statement.
- A brief history of your business.
- 2-3 paragraphs that summarize what your business is all about.
- Your logo, style guide, and any brand information.
- A listing of all the various software and systems you use to operate.
- Any business policies that you have, such as returns or booking changes.
- A list of past clients and a profile of what your perfect client or customer is like.
- Social Media Plan.

Potentially this is a lot of information and you may not want to assemble it all in one go. It can be helpful to first create an outline or notes document and write down things as they come to you. You can also start on a Monday and make a log of what you do during the week to use as prompts for content. Regardless of how long you take to create the document, ensure you keep it up to date as it will only create more questions if your Virtual Assistant doesn't have the correct information.

With a thorough business manual in place, your assistant will be able to get up to speed quickly and efficiently. This will only serve to benefit your business and give you more time to concentrate elsewhere.

ACTIVITY

As a reminder, in the back of this book you will find the workbook for all of the activities. As a book lover, I get that not everyone wants to permanently scribble on a page you have only one copy of. For this reason, you will find links that lead to both printable and fillable PDF pages for each activity.

Think about what it takes to run the day-to-day operations of your business and what others might need to know about it. Create an outline for your manual and a plan for adding information and completing it.

ORIENTATION

Let's welcome your new Virtual Assistant on board! It's orientation time!

After the contract is signed and you are ready to get started, the first thing you need to do is have an orientation. Start with a call or meeting that lasts a few hours and be sure you go through everything thoroughly. Once again, putting in the time now, is going to save you a lot of back and forth later.

Ahead of your call, send across any documents you want to go over, including your business manual, so that your assistant can prepare any questions ahead of time. Similarly, if you have any questions for them, such as contact preferences, working hours, etc., be sure to include those as well.

Along with your documents, provide an outline or agenda for the call. It's helpful for both parties to have a roadmap so that no one goes down a rabbit hole. Also leave time for questions or other aspects that come up as you are speaking – it might be helpful to appoint one of you as a note taker or share a live document such as

Google Docs or Dropbox Paper so you don't lose track.

During your conversation, ensure you speak about operations, projects, expectations, but also about the future. While it can be easy to map out your current plans and projects, you also want to give some insight into why these things matter. For instance, why is it crucial that your Social Media contain certain messaging, what will this help you to gain, where will it take your business?

You can also use this time to chat about goals or Key Performance Indicators (KPIs) that you have for each other. Each other? Yes, you did read that right. Your assistant may have goals for you as well. Sharing what you expect of each other is a great way to ensure your work is in sync and complimentary.

By taking the time to have a lengthy chat about your new relationship, you will ensure that you start off on the right foot, creating the foundation for a wonderful future working together.

ACTIVITY

As a reminder, in the back of this book you will find the workbook for all of the activities. As a book lover, I get that not everyone wants to permanently scribble on a page you have only one copy of. For this reason, you will find links that lead to both printable and fillable PDF pages for each activity.

Using your business manual (or outline) as a template, create a basic agenda for your orientation call. After you have made a note of the items you wish to discuss, estimate the time you will need for your chat. If it exceeds two hours, break it into a few sessions.

COMMUNICATION

Until this point, we have focused on finding your new wonderful and amazing virtual assistant (congrats, by the way!) – let's take some time to explore how you can maintain this relationship.

While lather rinsing and repeating is great for your hair, it isn't something you want to do with an assistant. The longer an assistant is with you, the more they learn and the more proficient they become. Over time, as proficiency builds, you may find that tasks are completed quicker allowing even more to be done in your time together.

In completing the previous activities, you will have created a wonderful basis for your relationship to thrive. There are, however, a few more things to take into consideration principle among them – communication.

We often hear the phrase, "Communication is key," and it is never more important than when interacting with someone you work with. Without proper communication, there may be frustration on both sides, which ultimately leads to a breakdown in work quality and motivation. In the next section we will take a look at how to effectively manage someone virtually, but for now, we will focus on honing your communication skills.

After the orientation phase, your assistant's head will likely be swimming with new information – remember that this is all new to them, whether they have had experience doing similar tasks, working with you and your business is uncharted territory. As I have mentioned before, it can take up to a year before a person fully adjusts to a new position and working relationship. You will need to nurture your time with them and ensure you remain open and flexible.

At the outset, communicating with your new assistant on a regular basis is key – weekly meetings being most common. During your orientation, ensure you set aside some time to talk about the frequency of your chats, how long you think you will need each week, and when they should be held. Scheduling ahead and on a consistent basis will help both of you in pacing your work, expectations, and give you a predictable timeline for reporting and follow-up. You may find it helpful to keep a shared running list between the two of you of items to speak about on your next call. Over time, depending on your work style, you may find that weekly meetings are not necessary -- it can vary from person to person and business to business. Do what it right for your assistant and yourself.

On an on-going basis, you will need a way to communicate regularly about projects and tasks. This will vary depending on the type of tool that works best for you and your assistant. No two people work in the exact same way; thus, it is important to utilize a system that works for both of you. A note of caution, that this can be a trial-and-error process, especially if you have never worked with an assistant or the implementation of a new organizational system was part of your overall goals when hiring. If you do try something and it isn't working, be open and honest with each other. Encourage your assistant to share if there is something they are struggling with and vice versa.

There are several popular solutions for project management communication, each with their own benefits and drawbacks, all depending on your work style and needs. Two of the most popular styles are bulletin boards – such as Trello and Asana – and collaborative documents such as Dropbox Paper and Google Drive (specifically Google Docs and Google Sheets).

The bulletin board style project management tools – Asana and Trello among them – are a wonderful way to track tasks, due dates, and assist in streamlining communication. These are both wonderful if you and your assistant are visual learners or like to go into a bit more detail than you might get on a standard list. There are also ways to expand these tools with add-ons or power-ups – turning an already advanced solution into a calendar, an automation, timeline, or full-blown CRM. Both tools are free for the basic versions and at a relatively low price point for the more advanced functions.

Collaborative document style management tools – such as Dropbox Paper and Google Drive – are a more basic way to keep track of tasks and progress; however, they are wonderful for projects that require the involvement of one or more persons. The main benefit, beyond the ability to have several people actively editing a document at one time, is that they are built into popular storage solutions. This means fewer logins and more things in one place (three cheers for that!). Both Google Docs and Google Sheets are well-known collaboration tools that exist within Google Drive and are available for free with any Google or Gmail account. Dropbox is also a popular storage solution, which now features (at the time of this writing) the ability to actively collaborate with Microsoft Documents. They also provide a much less known tool – Dropbox Paper – which assists in the creation of project management documents stored separately from your cloud files. While Dropbox

Paper is included with any Dropbox account, due to low storage limits, it is recommended to have an advanced plan.

Implementing regular communication and establishing a way to keep track of projects and tasks, is key to a successful working relationship with your assistant. Find what works for you both, even if it takes a little bit of time.

ACTIVITY

As a reminder, in the back of this book you will find the workbook for all of the activities. As a book lover, I get that not everyone wants to permanently scribble on a page you have only one copy of. For this reason, you will find links that lead to both printable and fillable PDF pages for each activity.

Take some time to think about how you best communicate (email, notes, phone call, face to face, etc.) and make a list of the aspects of organization that are helpful to you. Are you a visual learner? Do you love to make lists? Is writing things out in long form more your style? Use these answers to give you a head start on finding the right communication tools.

HOW TO EFFECTIVELY MANAGE SOMEONE VIRTUALLY

We've been through a lot together and hopefully you have learned some super awesome things about finding, hiring, and managing a virtual assistant! There's just one last aspect to go over – one that some might argue is the most important – management.

As with working styles, everyone has their own management style and in general no two are exactly the same. Let's face it, we have all had at least one experience where we felt we were managed incorrectly. The key to avoiding this? Acknowledging that your preferred management style may not mesh with your assistant and being able to change.

Over the course of this guide, you have had several opportunities to vet your applicant, talk to your new assistant, and get a feel for how you both might work together. Though it may seem perfect at the outset, some things, unfortunately, don't come to light until you have worked together. It may also be that this is your first time managing someone (or managing from afar) and not everyone slides into the role easily.

First and foremost, as mentioned in earlier sections, it is vitally important that you treat your relationship as you would a partnership. Without a doubt, you both have a stake in this venture and the person working with you is more than a casual employee. In particular, if you are a small business owner and your entire team consists of you and your assistant, you need to be on equal footing. This is no place for hierarchy or micro-management. Your assistant is there to make life easier and though it may take time to get things going, your goal is to be able to have greater flexibility. Your time should not be eaten up going over their work with a fine-tooth comb – have trust.

Ensuring that you have implemented the communication tools we talked about in the last section, is key to on-going effective management. This will allow you to manage expectations, have a clear organizational structure, and set milestones and due dates. Eliminating any surprises or unplanned last-minute tasks will go a long way in creating a more stable working relationship.

Additionally, creating an environment where your assistant feels valued and trusted is important. Being inconsistent or not letting them in on the big picture can cause irreparable damage. When you are relaying tasks be clear about the goals, outcome, and expectations – changing the project scope mid-stream or allowing a task that is no longer necessary to be completed, only leads to feelings of inadequacy. No one wants to feel as if the work that they are doing is pointless – create value for your assistant. When you plan out tasks be transparent about what the goal is, how it will affect the business, and what their role is. Ensure you are consistent in relaying information and moving things forward – value can also be found in completing a task or a project and moving on to the next stage.

Creating a welcoming environment for your assistant is also

important. Virtual work can be isolating and hard to navigate when you aren't in contact with someone every day, as you would be in an office. The psychological aspect of human isolation can be very damaging and ultimately affect a person's work and home life. What is the best way to combat this? First, be cognizant that you are working from a distance and implement face-to-face calls via Zoom or Skype. It is amazing how much difference it can make to see someone's face vs hearing their voice. You can also set aside a bit of time to talk about life in general – creating a report and establishing an outside link to the world. Why not celebrate accomplishments or take part in a virtual event together? You have goals, you can also have rewards when they are completed.

Similarly, take care to ensure you are both flexible and understanding. Chances are, if your assistant is only working for you a few hours a week, they will have other work to complete and, above all else, life happens. Being inflexible when someone has medical issues, a family emergency, or an unexpected event happens in their life can be disheartening and lead to feeling more like a number, less like a person. Giving your assistant time they need goes a long way toward building trust and a strong, lasting working relationship.

Being able to make your assistant feel valued, welcome, and as if they are a partner, are keys to managing a virtual relationship effectively. Be kind, consistent, and transparent and you will be well on your way to a creating a wonderful and amazing partnership for both you and your new kickass virtual assistant.

WORKBOOK: YOUR ACTIVITIES AWAIT!

TASKS ACTIVITY

To download and print a PDF copy of this activity or enroll in the online course visit http://bit.ly/FreeVirtualAssistantCourse.

There are three tasks for this activity.

1. Make a list of tasks that you currently don't have time for or those that you are thinking of implementing in the future. These can be as specific (creating graphics for social media) or as vague (data entry) as you want. Try to come up with at least 5.

2. Assign your tasks an estimated time for completion — remember this can be a range. Figure out your overall weekly need.

3. Estimate your overall budget and the number of hours that you might be able to fund. This can also be a range, as you will find varying pay rates and skill level in your search.

This page has been left blank. Use it to write, doodle, or make notes. Digital readers, just scroll on by my friends.

CREATING A KICK ASS AD ACTIVITY

To download and print a PDF copy of this activity or enroll in the online course visit http://bit.ly/FreeVirtualAssistantCourse.

Creating a fun and dynamic ad that is geared toward who you want to hire is key. Use the example and the tools in the workbook to create your own ad.

This page has been left blank. Use it to write, doodle, or make notes. Digital readers, just scroll on by my friends.

HOW TO PROPERLY VET APPLICATIONS ACTIVITY

To download and print a PDF copy of this activity or enroll in the online course visit http://bit.ly/FreeVirtualAssistantCourse.

Devise an evaluation matrix and system that allows you record, track, and evaluate your applicants. Ensure it allows you refer to it quickly and easily and above all else, that it makes your job easier, not more difficult.

This page has been left blank. Use it to write, doodle, or make notes.
Digital readers, just scroll on by my friends.

PRE-INTERVIEW CONTACT ACTIVITY

To download and print a PDF copy of this activity or enroll in the online course visit http://bit.ly/FreeVirtualAssistantCourse.

Create a template message that you will use during your interview communications. Ensure you have the minimum components included and try to make the content as dynamic and engaging as you can.

This page has been left blank. Use it to write, doodle, or make notes. Digital readers, just scroll on by my friends.

INTERVIEW QUESTIONS ACTIVITY

To download and print a PDF copy of this activity or enroll in the online course visit http://bit.ly/FreeVirtualAssistantCourse.

Create a set of 10 guiding questions for your interview, including 3 focusing on background, 3 on skill, 3 on fit, and the final one for the applicant to pose questions.

This page has been left blank. Use it to write, doodle, or make notes. Digital readers, just scroll on by my friends.

TESTING YOUR APPLICANTS ACTIVITY

To download and print a PDF copy of this activity or enroll in the online course visit http://bit.ly/FreeVirtualAssistantCourse.

Devise a test for your applicants that evaluates the relevant skills you need. Ensure the test measures the aspects that are important to you, such as speed, creativity, and presentation.

This page has been left blank. Use it to write, doodle, or make notes.
Digital readers, just scroll on by my friends.

POST-INTERVIEW CONTACT ACTIVITY

To download and print a PDF copy of this activity or enroll in the online course visit http://bit.ly/FreeVirtualAssistantCourse.

Create two templates for your post-interview follow-up – one for your new hire and one for those that didn't make the cut. Make the letters 2-3 paragraphs and be kind, courteous, and always thank them for their time (yes, even your new hire). For your new hire, carefully outline the next steps you want to take – scheduling a follow-up call, settling on a start date, and of course verifying a pay rate and contract.

This page has been left blank. Use it to write, doodle, or make notes. Digital readers, just scroll on by my friends.

CONTRACTS AND AGREEMENTS ACTIVITY

To download and print a PDF copy of this activity or enroll in the online course visit http://bit.ly/FreeVirtualAssistantCourse.

Create a template for a contract and an NDA (if you deem that one is necessary), using the information above. You can also find examples of complete contracts easily with an internet search and may get more ideas for additional elements to add. Second, create a list of preferences for yourself (such as paying bi-weekly) that you can use as the basis for your conversation with your new hire.

This page has been left blank. Use it to write, doodle, or make notes.
Digital readers, just scroll on by my friends.

BUSINESS MANUAL ACTIVITY

To download and print a PDF copy of this activity or enroll in the online course visit http://bit.ly/FreeVirtualAssistantCourse.

Think about what it takes to run the day-to-day operations of your business and what others might need to know about it. Create an outline for your manual and a plan for adding information and completing it.

This page has been left blank. Use it to write, doodle, or make notes.
Digital readers, just scroll on by my friends.

ORIENTATION ACTIVITY

To download and print a PDF copy of this activity or enroll in the online course visit http://bit.ly/FreeVirtualAssistantCourse.

Using your business manual (or outline) as a template, create a basic agenda for your orientation call. After you have made a note of the items you wish to discuss, estimate the time you will need for your chat. If it exceeds two hours, break it into a few sessions.

This page has been left blank. Use it to write, doodle, or make notes.
Digital readers, just scroll on by my friends.

COMMUNICATION ACTIVITY

To download and print a PDF copy of this activity or enroll in the online course visit http://bit.ly/FreeVirtualAssistantCourse.

Take some time to think about how you best communicate (email, notes, phone call, face to face, etc.) and make a list of the aspects of organization that are helpful to you. Are you a visual learner? Do you love to make lists? Is writing things out in long form more your style? Use these answers to give you a head start on finding the right communication tools.

This page has been left blank. Use it to write, doodle, or make notes.
Digital readers, just scroll on by my friends.

ABOUT THE AUTHOR

Charlene doesn't really like talking about herself much — an introvert to the core! She does enjoy cats, wine, snuggly socks and can often be found at home under her duvet.

She has worked in administrative capacities for her entire career and is currently the owner of a small creative consulting business — Panache Consulting.

In her previous lives, she received a Bachelors Degree in History from Northwestern University and a Masters in Cultural Heritage and International Development from the University of East Anglia.

• • •

Are you stuck or have questions? Give a shout (via email of course) and contact us at hello@thisispanache.com.

You can also visit the Panache Consulting website for PDF downloads and the accompanying video lessons at http://bit.ly/FreeVirtualAssistantCourse.

www.ingramcontent.com/pod-product-compliance
Lightning Source LLC
Chambersburg PA
CBHW070435220526
45466CB00004B/1686